50 Easy Baked Goods: From Cookies to Cakes

By: Kelly Johnson

Table of Contents

- Chocolate Chip Cookies
- Sugar Cookies
- Peanut Butter Cookies
- Oatmeal Raisin Cookies
- Snickerdoodles
- Gingerbread Cookies
- Brownies
- Blondies
- Chocolate Cake
- Vanilla Cupcakes
- Lemon Drizzle Cake
- Banana Bread
- Zucchini Bread
- Pumpkin Bread
- Coffee Cake
- Apple Pie
- Berry Crumble
- Cheesecake
- Carrot Cake
- Pound Cake
- Red Velvet Cake
- Chocolate Muffins
- Blueberry Muffins
- Cornbread
- Biscuits
- Scones
- Cinnamon Rolls
- Puff Pastry Twists
- Almond Biscotti
- Chocolate Eclairs
- Fruit Tarts
- Coconut Macaroons
- Peanut Butter Brownies
- Rice Krispie Treats
- Whoopie Pies
- Mini Cupcakes

- Chocolate Lava Cakes
- Tiramisu
- Molten Chocolate Cake
- Pumpkin Spice Muffins
- Sheet Pan Pancakes
- Fruit Galette
- Baklava
- Fudge Brownies
- Coffee Cake Muffins
- Shortbread Cookies
- Marshmallow Treats
- Chocolate Chip Banana Bread
- Strawberry Shortcake
- Oatmeal Chocolate Chip Cookies

Classic Chocolate Chip Cookies

Ingredients:

- **2 1/4 cups** all-purpose flour
- **1/2 teaspoon** baking soda
- **1 cup** unsalted butter, softened (2 sticks)
- **1/2 cup** granulated sugar
- **1 cup** packed brown sugar
- **1 teaspoon** salt
- **2 teaspoons** pure vanilla extract
- **2 large** eggs
- **2 cups** semisweet chocolate chips
- **1 cup** chopped nuts (optional)

Instructions:

1. **Preheat Oven:** Preheat your oven to 350°F (175°C). Line baking sheets with parchment paper.
2. **Mix Dry Ingredients:** In a small bowl, whisk together the flour and baking soda; set aside.
3. **Cream Butter and Sugars:** In a large bowl, beat the softened butter, granulated sugar, brown sugar, and salt together with a mixer on medium speed until smooth and creamy, about 2 minutes.
4. **Add Eggs and Vanilla:** Add the eggs, one at a time, mixing well after each addition. Then, mix in the vanilla extract.
5. **Combine Wet and Dry Ingredients:** Gradually blend in the flour mixture until just combined. Be careful not to overmix.
6. **Fold in Chocolate Chips:** Stir in the chocolate chips and nuts (if using) with a spatula or wooden spoon until evenly distributed.
7. **Scoop Dough:** Use a cookie scoop or tablespoon to drop rounded balls of dough onto the prepared baking sheets, spacing them about 2 inches apart.
8. **Bake:** Bake in the preheated oven for 9 to 11 minutes, or until the edges are golden brown but the centers are still soft.
9. **Cool:** Remove from the oven and let the cookies cool on the baking sheets for about 5 minutes before transferring them to wire racks to cool completely.

Sugar Cookies

Ingredients:

- **2 3/4 cups** all-purpose flour
- **1 teaspoon** baking soda
- **1/2 teaspoon** baking powder
- **1 cup** unsalted butter, softened
- **1 1/2 cups** granulated sugar
- **1 egg**
- **1 teaspoon** vanilla extract
- **1/2 teaspoon** almond extract (optional)
- **3/4 teaspoon** salt

Instructions:

1. Preheat oven to 375°F (190°C). In a small bowl, stir together flour, baking soda, baking powder, and salt; set aside.
2. In a large bowl, cream together the butter and sugar until smooth. Beat in the egg, vanilla, and almond extract.
3. Gradually blend in the dry ingredients. Roll rounded teaspoonfuls of dough into balls, and place onto ungreased cookie sheets.
4. Bake for 8 to 10 minutes, until golden. Let cool.

Peanut Butter Cookies

Ingredients:

- **1 cup** peanut butter
- **1 cup** granulated sugar
- **1 egg**
- **1 teaspoon** vanilla extract
- **1/2 teaspoon** baking soda
- **1/4 teaspoon** salt

Instructions:

1. Preheat oven to 350°F (175°C). In a bowl, mix all ingredients until smooth.
2. Roll dough into balls and place on a baking sheet. Flatten each ball with a fork, making a crisscross pattern.
3. Bake for 8 to 10 minutes, until edges are lightly browned. Let cool.

Oatmeal Raisin Cookies

Ingredients:

- **1 cup** unsalted butter, softened
- **1 cup** brown sugar, packed
- **1/2 cup** granulated sugar
- **2 large** eggs
- **1 teaspoon** vanilla extract
- **1 1/2 cups** all-purpose flour
- **1 teaspoon** baking soda
- **1 teaspoon** ground cinnamon
- **1/2 teaspoon** salt
- **3 cups** rolled oats
- **1 cup** raisins

Instructions:

1. Preheat oven to 350°F (175°C). Cream together the butter, brown sugar, and granulated sugar until smooth. Beat in the eggs and vanilla.
2. In another bowl, combine flour, baking soda, cinnamon, and salt; stir into the butter mixture. Mix in oats and raisins.
3. Drop by spoonfuls onto ungreased cookie sheets. Bake for 8 to 10 minutes. Cool on wire racks.

Snickerdoodles

Ingredients:

- **1 cup** unsalted butter, softened
- **1 1/2 cups** granulated sugar
- **2 large** eggs
- **2 3/4 cups** all-purpose flour
- **2 teaspoons** cream of tartar
- **1 teaspoon** baking soda
- **1/2 teaspoon** salt
- **3 tablespoons** sugar (for rolling)
- **1 tablespoon** ground cinnamon (for rolling)

Instructions:

1. Preheat oven to 400°F (200°C). Cream together butter and sugar until smooth. Beat in eggs.
2. In another bowl, combine flour, cream of tartar, baking soda, and salt. Gradually mix into the butter mixture.
3. Roll dough into balls, then roll in the cinnamon-sugar mixture. Place on ungreased cookie sheets.
4. Bake for 8 to 10 minutes until lightly browned. Let cool.

Gingerbread Cookies

Ingredients:

- **3 cups** all-purpose flour
- **1 teaspoon** baking soda
- **1 tablespoon** ground ginger
- **1 tablespoon** ground cinnamon
- **1/2 teaspoon** ground cloves
- **1/2 teaspoon** salt
- **1 cup** unsalted butter, softened
- **1 cup** brown sugar, packed
- **1/2 cup** molasses
- **1 large** egg

Instructions:

1. Preheat oven to 350°F (175°C). In a bowl, whisk together flour, baking soda, spices, and salt; set aside.
2. In another bowl, beat butter, brown sugar, molasses, and egg until smooth. Gradually blend in dry ingredients.
3. Roll out dough and cut into shapes. Place on ungreased baking sheets.
4. Bake for 8 to 10 minutes. Cool completely.

Brownies

Ingredients:

- **1/2 cup** unsalted butter
- **1 cup** granulated sugar
- **2 large** eggs
- **1 teaspoon** vanilla extract
- **1/3 cup** unsweetened cocoa powder
- **1/2 cup** all-purpose flour
- **1/4 teaspoon** salt
- **1/4 teaspoon** baking powder

Instructions:

1. Preheat oven to 350°F (175°C). Melt butter and mix with sugar, eggs, and vanilla.
2. In another bowl, mix cocoa, flour, salt, and baking powder; stir into the wet mixture until blended.
3. Spread into a greased 8x8-inch baking pan. Bake for 20 to 25 minutes. Cool and cut into squares.

Blondies

Ingredients:

- **1/2 cup** unsalted butter, melted
- **1 cup** brown sugar, packed
- **1/4 cup** granulated sugar
- **1 large** egg
- **1 teaspoon** vanilla extract
- **1 1/2 cups** all-purpose flour
- **1/2 teaspoon** baking powder
- **1/4 teaspoon** salt
- **1 cup** chocolate chips or nuts (optional)

Instructions:

1. Preheat oven to 350°F (175°C). In a bowl, mix melted butter with brown sugar and granulated sugar until smooth. Beat in egg and vanilla.
2. Stir in flour, baking powder, and salt until just combined. Fold in chocolate chips or nuts if desired.
3. Spread into a greased 8x8-inch baking pan. Bake for 20 to 25 minutes. Cool and cut into squares.

Chocolate Cake

Ingredients:

- **1 3/4 cups** all-purpose flour
- **3/4 cup** unsweetened cocoa powder
- **2 cups** granulated sugar
- **1 1/2 teaspoons** baking powder
- **1 1/2 teaspoons** baking soda
- **1 teaspoon** salt
- **2 large** eggs
- **1 cup** whole milk
- **1/2 cup** vegetable oil
- **2 teaspoons** vanilla extract
- **1 cup** boiling water

Instructions:

1. Preheat oven to 350°F (175°C). Grease and flour two 9-inch round cake pans.
2. In a large bowl, mix flour, cocoa powder, sugar, baking powder, baking soda, and salt. Add eggs, milk, oil, and vanilla; mix for 2 minutes on medium speed.
3. Stir in boiling water (batter will be thin). Pour evenly into prepared pans.
4. Bake for 30 to 35 minutes. Cool in pans for 10 minutes, then remove to wire racks to cool completely.

Vanilla Cupcakes

Ingredients:

- **1 1/2 cups** all-purpose flour
- **1 cup** granulated sugar
- **1/2 cup** unsalted butter, softened
- **2 large** eggs
- **1/2 cup** milk
- **2 teaspoons** vanilla extract
- **1 1/2 teaspoons** baking powder
- **1/4 teaspoon** salt

Instructions:

1. Preheat oven to 350°F (175°C). Line a muffin tin with cupcake liners.
2. In a large bowl, cream together the butter and sugar until light and fluffy. Beat in the eggs, one at a time, then stir in the vanilla.
3. In another bowl, combine flour, baking powder, and salt. Gradually add to the creamed mixture alternately with milk, mixing well after each addition.
4. Fill cupcake liners about two-thirds full. Bake for 15 to 20 minutes, or until a toothpick comes out clean. Let cool before frosting.

Lemon Drizzle Cake

Ingredients:

- **1 1/2 cups** all-purpose flour
- **1 cup** granulated sugar
- **1/2 cup** unsalted butter, softened
- **2 large** eggs
- **1/2 cup** milk
- **1 tablespoon** lemon zest
- **1/4 cup** lemon juice
- **1 teaspoon** baking powder
- **1/2 teaspoon** salt

Instructions:

1. Preheat oven to 350°F (175°C). Grease a loaf pan.
2. In a bowl, cream together butter and sugar until light and fluffy. Beat in eggs, lemon zest, and lemon juice.
3. In another bowl, mix flour, baking powder, and salt. Gradually add dry ingredients to the wet mixture, alternating with milk.
4. Pour into the prepared loaf pan and bake for 50 to 60 minutes. Let cool, then drizzle with a mixture of powdered sugar and lemon juice.

Banana Bread

Ingredients:

- **2 to 3** ripe bananas, mashed
- **1/3 cup** melted butter
- **3/4 cup** granulated sugar
- **1 large** egg, beaten
- **1 teaspoon** vanilla extract
- **1 teaspoon** baking soda
- **Pinch of salt**
- **1 1/2 cups** all-purpose flour

Instructions:

1. Preheat oven to 350°F (175°C). Grease a 4x8-inch loaf pan.
2. In a mixing bowl, mix mashed bananas with melted butter. Stir in sugar, beaten egg, and vanilla.
3. Sprinkle baking soda and salt over the mixture and mix in. Add flour and stir until just combined.
4. Pour batter into the prepared pan. Bake for 60 to 65 minutes. Cool in the pan for 10 minutes before transferring to a wire rack.

Zucchini Bread

Ingredients:

- **1 1/2 cups** grated zucchini
- **1/2 cup** unsalted butter, melted
- **1 cup** granulated sugar
- **2 large** eggs
- **1 teaspoon** vanilla extract
- **1 1/2 cups** all-purpose flour
- **1 teaspoon** baking soda
- **1/2 teaspoon** baking powder
- **1/2 teaspoon** salt
- **1 teaspoon** ground cinnamon

Instructions:

1. Preheat oven to 350°F (175°C). Grease a loaf pan.
2. In a bowl, mix grated zucchini with melted butter. Stir in sugar, eggs, and vanilla.
3. In another bowl, combine flour, baking soda, baking powder, salt, and cinnamon. Gradually add to the wet ingredients until just combined.
4. Pour batter into the prepared loaf pan. Bake for 50 to 60 minutes. Let cool before slicing.

Pumpkin Bread

Ingredients:

- **1 3/4 cups** all-purpose flour
- **1 cup** sugar
- **1/2 cup** unsalted butter, softened
- **1 cup** pumpkin puree
- **2 large** eggs
- **1 teaspoon** baking soda
- **1/2 teaspoon** baking powder
- **1 teaspoon** cinnamon
- **1/2 teaspoon** nutmeg
- **1/2 teaspoon** salt

Instructions:

1. Preheat oven to 350°F (175°C). Grease a loaf pan.
2. In a bowl, cream together the butter and sugar. Beat in the eggs and pumpkin puree until smooth.
3. In another bowl, mix flour, baking soda, baking powder, spices, and salt. Gradually add to the wet mixture, stirring until just combined.
4. Pour into the prepared pan and bake for 60 to 70 minutes. Cool before removing from the pan.

Coffee Cake

Ingredients:

- **2 cups** all-purpose flour
- **1 cup** granulated sugar
- **1/2 cup** unsalted butter, softened
- **1 cup** sour cream
- **2 large** eggs
- **1 teaspoon** baking powder
- **1/2 teaspoon** baking soda
- **1 teaspoon** vanilla extract
- **1 teaspoon** cinnamon (for the topping)
- **1/4 cup** brown sugar (for the topping)

Instructions:

1. Preheat oven to 350°F (175°C). Grease a 9-inch round cake pan.
2. In a bowl, cream together butter and sugar until fluffy. Beat in eggs, sour cream, and vanilla.
3. In another bowl, mix flour, baking powder, baking soda, and cinnamon. Gradually add dry ingredients to the wet mixture until just combined.
4. Pour batter into the pan. Mix brown sugar and cinnamon and sprinkle on top. Bake for 30 to 35 minutes. Let cool before serving.

Apple Pie

Ingredients:

- **6 to 8** apples, peeled and sliced
- **3/4 cup** granulated sugar
- **2 tablespoons** all-purpose flour
- **1 teaspoon** cinnamon
- **1 tablespoon** lemon juice
- **1 tablespoon** butter
- **1 package** pie crusts (store-bought or homemade)

Instructions:

1. Preheat oven to 425°F (220°C). Roll out one pie crust and place in a pie pan.
2. In a bowl, combine sliced apples with sugar, flour, cinnamon, and lemon juice.
3. Pour apple mixture into the crust and dot with butter. Cover with the second pie crust, sealing the edges.
4. Cut slits in the top crust to allow steam to escape. Bake for 15 minutes, then reduce temperature to 350°F (175°C) and bake for an additional 35 to 45 minutes. Cool before serving.

Berry Crumble

Ingredients:

- **4 cups** mixed berries (strawberries, blueberries, raspberries)
- **1/2 cup** granulated sugar
- **1 tablespoon** lemon juice
- **1 cup** rolled oats
- **1/2 cup** all-purpose flour
- **1/2 cup** brown sugar
- **1/2 cup** unsalted butter, melted
- **1 teaspoon** cinnamon

Instructions:

1. Preheat oven to 350°F (175°C). In a bowl, toss mixed berries with sugar and lemon juice. Pour into a baking dish.
2. In another bowl, combine oats, flour, brown sugar, melted butter, and cinnamon until crumbly.
3. Sprinkle oat mixture over the berries. Bake for 30 to 35 minutes, until bubbly and golden. Serve warm.

Cheesecake

Ingredients:

- **1 1/2 cups** graham cracker crumbs
- **1/4 cup** granulated sugar
- **1/2 cup** unsalted butter, melted
- **4 (8-ounce)** packages cream cheese, softened
- **1 cup** granulated sugar
- **1 teaspoon** vanilla extract
- **4 large** eggs
- **1 cup** sour cream

Instructions:

1. Preheat oven to 325°F (160°C). Grease a 9-inch springform pan.
2. In a bowl, mix graham cracker crumbs, sugar, and melted butter. Press mixture into the bottom of the prepared pan.
3. In another bowl, beat cream cheese until smooth. Gradually add sugar and vanilla, mixing well. Add eggs, one at a time, mixing after each addition.
4. Pour filling over the crust. Bake for 55-60 minutes. Let cool, then refrigerate for at least 4 hours before serving.

Carrot Cake

Ingredients:

- **2 cups** all-purpose flour
- **2 cups** granulated sugar
- **1 teaspoon** baking powder
- **1 teaspoon** baking soda
- **1 teaspoon** ground cinnamon
- **1/2 teaspoon** salt
- **1 cup** vegetable oil
- **4 large** eggs
- **3 cups** grated carrots
- **1 cup** crushed pineapple, drained
- **1 cup** chopped walnuts (optional)

Instructions:

1. Preheat oven to 350°F (175°C). Grease and flour two 9-inch round cake pans.
2. In a large bowl, mix flour, sugar, baking powder, baking soda, cinnamon, and salt.
3. In another bowl, whisk together oil and eggs. Stir in carrots, pineapple, and walnuts. Add to dry ingredients and mix until just combined.
4. Divide batter between the prepared pans and bake for 30 to 35 minutes. Cool in pans for 10 minutes, then transfer to wire racks to cool completely.

Pound Cake

Ingredients:

- **2 cups** unsalted butter, softened
- **2 cups** granulated sugar
- **8 large** eggs
- **3 cups** all-purpose flour
- **1 teaspoon** vanilla extract
- **1 teaspoon** almond extract
- **1/4 teaspoon** salt

Instructions:

1. Preheat oven to 325°F (160°C). Grease a 10-inch bundt pan.
2. In a large bowl, cream butter and sugar until light and fluffy. Add eggs, one at a time, mixing well after each addition.
3. Gradually add flour, mixing just until combined. Stir in vanilla, almond extract, and salt.
4. Pour batter into the prepared bundt pan and bake for 1 hour or until a toothpick comes out clean. Let cool before removing from the pan.

Red Velvet Cake

Ingredients:

- **2 1/2 cups** all-purpose flour
- **1 1/2 cups** granulated sugar
- **1 teaspoon** baking soda
- **1 teaspoon** salt
- **1 teaspoon** cocoa powder
- **1 1/2 cups** vegetable oil
- **1 cup** buttermilk
- **2 large** eggs
- **2 tablespoons** red food coloring
- **1 teaspoon** vanilla extract
- **1 teaspoon** white vinegar

Instructions:

1. Preheat oven to 350°F (175°C). Grease and flour two 9-inch round cake pans.
2. In a bowl, mix flour, sugar, baking soda, salt, and cocoa powder.
3. In another bowl, mix oil, buttermilk, eggs, food coloring, vanilla, and vinegar. Add to the dry ingredients and mix until smooth.
4. Divide batter between the prepared pans and bake for 25 to 30 minutes. Cool in pans for 10 minutes, then transfer to wire racks.

Chocolate Muffins

Ingredients:

- **1 3/4 cups** all-purpose flour
- **1 cup** granulated sugar
- **1/2 cup** unsweetened cocoa powder
- **1 teaspoon** baking soda
- **1/2 teaspoon** salt
- **1/2 cup** vegetable oil
- **2 large** eggs
- **1 cup** milk
- **1 teaspoon** vanilla extract
- **1 cup** chocolate chips

Instructions:

1. Preheat oven to 350°F (175°C). Line a muffin tin with paper liners.
2. In a bowl, mix flour, sugar, cocoa powder, baking soda, and salt.
3. In another bowl, whisk together oil, eggs, milk, and vanilla. Add to the dry ingredients and stir until just combined. Fold in chocolate chips.
4. Fill muffin cups about 2/3 full and bake for 18 to 20 minutes. Let cool before serving.

Blueberry Muffins

Ingredients:

- **2 cups** all-purpose flour
- **1/2 cup** granulated sugar
- **2 teaspoons** baking powder
- **1/2 teaspoon** baking soda
- **1/2 teaspoon** salt
- **1/2 cup** unsalted butter, melted
- **2 large** eggs
- **1 cup** milk
- **1 teaspoon** vanilla extract
- **1 1/2 cups** fresh blueberries

Instructions:

1. Preheat oven to 375°F (190°C). Line a muffin tin with paper liners.
2. In a bowl, mix flour, sugar, baking powder, baking soda, and salt.
3. In another bowl, whisk together melted butter, eggs, milk, and vanilla. Add to dry ingredients and mix until just combined. Fold in blueberries.
4. Fill muffin cups about 2/3 full and bake for 20 to 25 minutes. Let cool before serving.

Cornbread

Ingredients:

- **1 cup** cornmeal
- **1 cup** all-purpose flour
- **1/4 cup** granulated sugar
- **1 tablespoon** baking powder
- **1/2 teaspoon** salt
- **1 cup** milk
- **1/4 cup** unsalted butter, melted
- **2 large** eggs

Instructions:

1. Preheat oven to 400°F (200°C). Grease an 8-inch square baking pan.
2. In a bowl, mix cornmeal, flour, sugar, baking powder, and salt.
3. In another bowl, whisk together milk, melted butter, and eggs. Add to dry ingredients and stir until just combined.
4. Pour batter into the prepared pan and bake for 20 to 25 minutes, until golden brown. Let cool before cutting into squares.

Biscuits

Ingredients:

- **2 cups** all-purpose flour
- **1 tablespoon** baking powder
- **1/2 teaspoon** salt
- **1/4 cup** unsalted butter, cold and cubed
- **3/4 cup** milk

Instructions:

1. Preheat oven to 450°F (230°C). Line a baking sheet with parchment paper.
2. In a bowl, mix flour, baking powder, and salt. Cut in butter until mixture resembles coarse crumbs.
3. Stir in milk until just combined. Do not overmix.
4. Turn dough onto a floured surface and gently knead a few times. Roll out to 1-inch thickness and cut out biscuits. Place on the prepared baking sheet.
5. Bake for 12 to 15 minutes, until golden brown. Serve warm.

Scones

Ingredients:

- **2 cups** all-purpose flour
- **1/4 cup** granulated sugar
- **1 tablespoon** baking powder
- **1/2 teaspoon** salt
- **1/2 cup** unsalted butter, cold and cubed
- **1/2 cup** milk
- **1 large** egg
- **1 teaspoon** vanilla extract
- Optional: **1 cup** dried fruit or chocolate chips

Instructions:

1. Preheat oven to 400°F (200°C). Line a baking sheet with parchment paper.
2. In a bowl, whisk together flour, sugar, baking powder, and salt. Cut in butter until mixture resembles coarse crumbs.
3. In another bowl, whisk together milk, egg, and vanilla. Stir into dry ingredients until just combined. Fold in any optional ingredients.
4. Turn dough onto a floured surface, knead gently, and pat into a circle about 1-inch thick. Cut into wedges or use a round cutter.
5. Place on the prepared baking sheet and bake for 15-20 minutes until golden brown. Serve warm.

Cinnamon Rolls

Ingredients:

- **4 cups** all-purpose flour
- **1/4 cup** granulated sugar
- **1 packet (2 1/4 teaspoons)** instant yeast
- **1 teaspoon** salt
- **1 cup** milk, warmed
- **1/4 cup** unsalted butter, melted
- **2 large** eggs
- **1/2 cup** brown sugar
- **2 tablespoons** ground cinnamon
- **1/4 cup** unsalted butter, softened (for filling)
- Optional: **1 cup** powdered sugar (for icing)

Instructions:

1. In a bowl, mix flour, sugar, yeast, and salt. In another bowl, combine warm milk, melted butter, and eggs. Add to dry ingredients and mix until a dough forms.
2. Knead dough on a floured surface until smooth. Let rise in a warm place until doubled in size, about 1 hour.
3. Roll out dough into a rectangle. Spread softened butter over the surface, sprinkle with brown sugar and cinnamon.
4. Roll tightly and cut into slices. Place in a greased baking dish and let rise for another 30 minutes.
5. Preheat oven to 375°F (190°C) and bake for 20-25 minutes. If desired, mix powdered sugar with a little milk for icing and drizzle over warm rolls.

Puff Pastry Twists

Ingredients:

- **1 package** frozen puff pastry (2 sheets), thawed
- **1/2 cup** grated cheese (like cheddar or parmesan)
- **1/2 teaspoon** garlic powder
- **1/2 teaspoon** paprika
- **1 egg** (for egg wash)
- **Salt and pepper to taste**

Instructions:

1. Preheat oven to 400°F (200°C). Line a baking sheet with parchment paper.
2. Roll out each puff pastry sheet on a floured surface. Cut each sheet into strips about 1 inch wide.
3. In a bowl, mix cheese, garlic powder, paprika, salt, and pepper. Sprinkle mixture over half of each strip.
4. Fold the strips in half and twist them. Place on the baking sheet.
5. Beat the egg and brush over each twist. Bake for 15-20 minutes until golden brown. Serve warm.

Almond Biscotti

Ingredients:

- **2 cups** all-purpose flour
- **1 cup** granulated sugar
- **1/2 teaspoon** baking powder
- **1/4 teaspoon** salt
- **3 large** eggs
- **1 teaspoon** vanilla extract
- **1 teaspoon** almond extract
- **1 cup** sliced almonds

Instructions:

1. Preheat oven to 350°F (175°C). Line a baking sheet with parchment paper.
2. In a bowl, mix flour, sugar, baking powder, and salt. In another bowl, whisk together eggs, vanilla, and almond extract.
3. Gradually add the wet ingredients to the dry ingredients. Stir in almonds.
4. Shape the dough into a log and place on the prepared baking sheet. Bake for 25-30 minutes until golden.
5. Let cool slightly, then slice into individual pieces. Bake slices for an additional 10-15 minutes until crisp.

Chocolate Eclairs

Ingredients:

- **1 cup** water
- **1/2 cup** unsalted butter
- **1 cup** all-purpose flour
- **4 large** eggs
- **1/2 cup** heavy cream (for filling)
- **1 cup** powdered sugar (for icing)
- **3 tablespoons** cocoa powder (for icing)

Instructions:

1. Preheat oven to 400°F (200°C). Line a baking sheet with parchment paper.
2. In a saucepan, bring water and butter to a boil. Stir in flour until the mixture forms a ball. Remove from heat and let cool slightly.
3. Add eggs, one at a time, mixing well after each addition. Drop or pipe onto the baking sheet in 4-inch lines.
4. Bake for 20-25 minutes until puffed and golden. Let cool completely.
5. Whip heavy cream and fill the cooled eclairs. For icing, mix powdered sugar and cocoa powder with a little water to make a glaze and dip the tops of the eclairs.

Fruit Tarts

Ingredients:

- **1 1/2 cups** all-purpose flour
- **1/2 cup** unsalted butter, softened
- **1/4 cup** powdered sugar
- **1 large** egg yolk
- **1/2 teaspoon** vanilla extract
- **1 cup** pastry cream (store-bought or homemade)
- **Assorted fresh fruits** (such as berries, kiwi, and bananas)
- **1/4 cup** apricot jam (for glaze)

Instructions:

1. Preheat oven to 350°F (175°C). Grease tart pans.
2. In a bowl, mix flour, butter, powdered sugar, egg yolk, and vanilla until a dough forms. Press into tart pans.
3. Bake for 15-20 minutes until golden. Let cool.
4. Fill cooled tart shells with pastry cream and arrange fresh fruits on top.
5. Heat apricot jam until melted and brush over the fruit for glaze.

Coconut Macaroons

Ingredients:

- **3 cups** shredded coconut
- **1/2 cup** sweetened condensed milk
- **1 teaspoon** vanilla extract
- **2 large** egg whites
- **1/4 teaspoon** salt
- **1/2 cup** chocolate chips (optional for dipping)

Instructions:

1. Preheat oven to 325°F (165°C). Line a baking sheet with parchment paper.
2. In a bowl, combine coconut, sweetened condensed milk, and vanilla. In another bowl, whip egg whites with salt until stiff peaks form.
3. Gently fold egg whites into the coconut mixture.
4. Drop tablespoon-sized mounds onto the prepared baking sheet. Bake for 20-25 minutes until golden.
5. If desired, melt chocolate chips and dip the bottoms of the cooled macaroons in chocolate.

Peanut Butter Brownies

Ingredients:

- **1/2 cup** unsalted butter
- **1 cup** granulated sugar
- **2 large** eggs
- **1 teaspoon** vanilla extract
- **1/2 cup** all-purpose flour
- **1/3 cup** cocoa powder
- **1/4 teaspoon** salt
- **1/2 cup** creamy peanut butter

Instructions:

1. Preheat oven to 350°F (175°C). Grease an 8x8-inch baking pan.
2. In a saucepan, melt butter over low heat. Remove from heat and stir in sugar, eggs, and vanilla.
3. Add flour, cocoa powder, and salt; mix until just combined. Pour into the prepared pan.
4. Drop spoonfuls of peanut butter over the brownie batter and swirl with a knife.
5. Bake for 20-25 minutes until a toothpick comes out clean. Let cool before cutting into squares.

Rice Krispie Treats

Ingredients:

- **3 tablespoons** unsalted butter
- **1 package (10 oz)** mini marshmallows
- **6 cups** Rice Krispies cereal

Instructions:

1. In a large saucepan, melt butter over low heat. Add marshmallows and stir until completely melted and smooth.
2. Remove from heat and add Rice Krispies. Stir until well coated.
3. Press the mixture into a greased 9x13-inch pan. Allow to cool, then cut into squares.

Whoopie Pies

Ingredients:

- **1 1/2 cups** all-purpose flour
- **1/2 cup** unsweetened cocoa powder
- **1 teaspoon** baking powder
- **1/2 teaspoon** baking soda
- **1/4 teaspoon** salt
- **1/2 cup** unsalted butter, softened
- **1 cup** granulated sugar
- **1 large** egg
- **1 teaspoon** vanilla extract
- **1 cup** milk
- **Filling:** 1 cup marshmallow fluff, 1/2 cup powdered sugar, and 1/4 cup unsalted butter, softened

Instructions:

1. Preheat oven to 350°F (175°C). Line a baking sheet with parchment paper.
2. In a bowl, mix flour, cocoa, baking powder, baking soda, and salt. In another bowl, beat butter and sugar until fluffy. Add egg and vanilla; mix well.
3. Gradually add dry ingredients to the wet mixture, alternating with milk. Drop tablespoons of batter onto the prepared baking sheet.
4. Bake for 10-12 minutes until springy. Let cool completely.
5. For the filling, beat marshmallow fluff, powdered sugar, and butter until smooth. Spread between two cookies to make sandwiches.

Mini Cupcakes

Ingredients:

- **1 cup** all-purpose flour
- **1/2 cup** granulated sugar
- **1/2 teaspoon** baking powder
- **1/4 teaspoon** baking soda
- **1/4 teaspoon** salt
- **1/4 cup** unsalted butter, softened
- **1/2 cup** buttermilk
- **1 large** egg
- **1 teaspoon** vanilla extract

Instructions:

1. Preheat oven to 350°F (175°C). Line a mini cupcake pan with paper liners.
2. In a bowl, combine flour, sugar, baking powder, baking soda, and salt. In another bowl, beat butter, buttermilk, egg, and vanilla until smooth.
3. Gradually add dry ingredients to the wet mixture and stir until combined.
4. Fill each mini cupcake liner about two-thirds full. Bake for 12-15 minutes until a toothpick comes out clean. Let cool before frosting.

Chocolate Lava Cakes

Ingredients:

- **1/2 cup** unsalted butter
- **1 cup** semi-sweet chocolate chips
- **2 large** eggs
- **2 large** egg yolks
- **1/4 cup** granulated sugar
- **2 tablespoons** all-purpose flour
- Optional: powdered sugar and berries for serving

Instructions:

1. Preheat oven to 425°F (220°C). Grease four ramekins and place them on a baking sheet.
2. In a saucepan, melt butter and chocolate chips over low heat until smooth. Remove from heat and let cool slightly.
3. In a bowl, whisk eggs, egg yolks, and sugar until thick. Stir in the chocolate mixture and flour until combined.
4. Divide the batter among the ramekins and bake for 12-14 minutes until the edges are firm but the center is soft.
5. Let cool for 1 minute, then invert onto plates. Dust with powdered sugar and serve with berries.

Tiramisu

Ingredients:

- **1 cup** strong brewed coffee, cooled
- **1 tablespoon** coffee liqueur (optional)
- **3 large** eggs, separated
- **1/2 cup** granulated sugar
- **1 cup** mascarpone cheese
- **1 cup** heavy cream
- **1 package (7 oz)** ladyfinger cookies
- **Cocoa powder for dusting**

Instructions:

1. In a bowl, combine coffee and coffee liqueur. In another bowl, beat egg yolks and sugar until pale and thick. Stir in mascarpone until smooth.
2. In a separate bowl, whip cream to soft peaks, then fold into the mascarpone mixture.
3. Dip each ladyfinger briefly in the coffee mixture and layer them in a dish. Spread half of the mascarpone mixture over the ladyfingers.
4. Repeat with another layer of dipped ladyfingers and the remaining mascarpone mixture. Cover and refrigerate for at least 4 hours or overnight.
5. Dust with cocoa powder before serving.

Molten Chocolate Cake

Ingredients:

- **1/2 cup** unsalted butter
- **1 cup** semi-sweet chocolate chips
- **2 large** eggs
- **2 large** egg yolks
- **1/4 cup** granulated sugar
- **2 tablespoons** all-purpose flour
- Optional: powdered sugar and ice cream for serving

Instructions:

1. Preheat oven to 425°F (220°C). Grease four ramekins and place them on a baking sheet.
2. In a microwave-safe bowl, melt butter and chocolate chips until smooth, stirring frequently.
3. In another bowl, whisk eggs, egg yolks, and sugar until thick. Stir in the chocolate mixture and flour until combined.
4. Divide the batter among the ramekins and bake for 12-14 minutes until the edges are firm but the center is soft.
5. Let cool for 1 minute, then invert onto plates. Dust with powdered sugar and serve with ice cream.

Pumpkin Spice Muffins

Ingredients:

- **1 1/2 cups** all-purpose flour
- **1 teaspoon** baking powder
- **1 teaspoon** baking soda
- **1 teaspoon** ground cinnamon
- **1/2 teaspoon** ground nutmeg
- **1/2 teaspoon** ground ginger
- **1/4 teaspoon** salt
- **1/2 cup** vegetable oil
- **1 cup** canned pumpkin puree
- **3/4 cup** granulated sugar
- **2 large** eggs

Instructions:

1. Preheat oven to 350°F (175°C). Line a muffin tin with paper liners.
2. In a bowl, combine flour, baking powder, baking soda, spices, and salt. In another bowl, whisk together oil, pumpkin, sugar, and eggs until smooth.
3. Gradually add dry ingredients to the wet mixture and stir until just combined.
4. Fill each muffin liner about two-thirds full. Bake for 18-20 minutes until a toothpick comes out clean. Let cool before serving.

Sheet Pan Pancakes

Ingredients:

- **2 cups** all-purpose flour
- **2 tablespoons** sugar
- **1 tablespoon** baking powder
- **1/2 teaspoon** salt
- **2 cups** milk
- **1/4 cup** melted butter
- **2 large** eggs
- Optional: berries or chocolate chips for topping

Instructions:

1. Preheat oven to 425°F (220°C). Grease a rimmed baking sheet.
2. In a bowl, mix flour, sugar, baking powder, and salt. In another bowl, whisk together milk, melted butter, and eggs.
3. Gradually add the wet ingredients to the dry ingredients and stir until just combined.
4. Pour the batter onto the prepared baking sheet and spread evenly. Top with berries or chocolate chips if desired.
5. Bake for 15-20 minutes until golden and set. Cut into squares and serve with syrup.

Fruit Galette

Ingredients:

- **1 1/4 cups** all-purpose flour
- **1/4 teaspoon** salt
- **1/2 cup** unsalted butter, chilled and diced
- **1/4 cup** ice water
- **2 cups** mixed fresh fruit (e.g., berries, peaches, apples)
- **1/4 cup** granulated sugar
- **1 tablespoon** cornstarch
- **1 teaspoon** vanilla extract
- **1 egg** (for egg wash)
- **1 tablespoon** coarse sugar (for topping)

Instructions:

1. In a bowl, combine flour and salt. Cut in butter until the mixture resembles coarse crumbs. Stir in ice water until the dough forms a ball. Wrap in plastic and refrigerate for 30 minutes.
2. Preheat the oven to 375°F (190°C). Roll out the dough on a floured surface into a 12-inch circle.
3. In another bowl, toss the fruit with sugar, cornstarch, and vanilla. Place the fruit mixture in the center of the dough, leaving a 2-inch border.
4. Fold the edges of the dough over the fruit, pleating as necessary. Brush the dough with beaten egg and sprinkle with coarse sugar.
5. Bake for 35-40 minutes until the crust is golden and the fruit is bubbly. Let cool slightly before serving.

Baklava

Ingredients:

- **1 package (16 oz)** phyllo dough, thawed
- **2 cups** walnuts or pistachios, finely chopped
- **1 teaspoon** ground cinnamon
- **1 cup** unsalted butter, melted
- **1 cup** granulated sugar
- **1 cup** water
- **1/2 cup** honey
- **1 teaspoon** vanilla extract

Instructions:

1. Preheat the oven to 350°F (175°C). In a bowl, combine nuts and cinnamon.
2. Grease a 9x13-inch baking dish. Layer 8 sheets of phyllo dough in the dish, brushing each layer with melted butter. Sprinkle a layer of nut mixture, then add 2 more phyllo sheets, buttering each.
3. Repeat layers, alternating between nuts and phyllo, until all nuts are used. Top with 8 more layers of phyllo, buttering each.
4. Cut the baklava into diamond shapes. Bake for 45-50 minutes until golden.
5. In a saucepan, combine sugar, water, honey, and vanilla. Boil for 10 minutes. Pour over the hot baklava. Let cool before serving.

Fudge Brownies

Ingredients:

- **1/2 cup** unsalted butter
- **1 cup** granulated sugar
- **2 large** eggs
- **1 teaspoon** vanilla extract
- **1/3 cup** unsweetened cocoa powder
- **1/2 cup** all-purpose flour
- **1/4 teaspoon** salt
- **1/4 teaspoon** baking powder

Instructions:

1. Preheat the oven to 350°F (175°C). Grease an 8x8-inch baking pan.
2. In a saucepan, melt butter. Remove from heat and stir in sugar, eggs, and vanilla until well combined.
3. Mix in cocoa powder, flour, salt, and baking powder until just combined.
4. Pour the batter into the prepared pan and spread evenly. Bake for 20-25 minutes until a toothpick comes out with moist crumbs. Let cool before cutting into squares.

Coffee Cake Muffins

Ingredients:

- **1 1/2 cups** all-purpose flour
- **1 teaspoon** baking powder
- **1/2 teaspoon** baking soda
- **1/2 teaspoon** salt
- **1/2 teaspoon** ground cinnamon
- **1/2 cup** unsalted butter, softened
- **1 cup** granulated sugar
- **2 large** eggs
- **1 teaspoon** vanilla extract
- **1/2 cup** sour cream
- **1/2 cup** brown sugar
- **1/4 cup** chopped nuts (optional)
- **1/2 teaspoon** ground cinnamon (for topping)

Instructions:

1. Preheat the oven to 350°F (175°C). Line a muffin tin with paper liners.
2. In a bowl, mix flour, baking powder, baking soda, salt, and cinnamon. In another bowl, cream together butter and sugar until light and fluffy. Beat in eggs, one at a time, then stir in vanilla.
3. Mix in the dry ingredients alternately with sour cream until just combined.
4. In a small bowl, combine brown sugar, nuts, and cinnamon for the topping.
5. Fill each muffin liner halfway with batter, sprinkle with the topping, then add more batter on top. Bake for 18-20 minutes until a toothpick comes out clean. Let cool before serving.

Shortbread Cookies

Ingredients:

- **1 cup** unsalted butter, softened
- **1/2 cup** granulated sugar
- **1/4 teaspoon** salt
- **2 cups** all-purpose flour
- **1 teaspoon** vanilla extract

Instructions:

1. Preheat the oven to 350°F (175°C). Line a baking sheet with parchment paper.
2. In a large bowl, cream together the butter, sugar, and salt until smooth. Stir in the vanilla extract.
3. Gradually add the flour, mixing until just combined.
4. Roll the dough into a log and slice into rounds or shape into desired forms.
5. Place on the prepared baking sheet and bake for 12-15 minutes, or until lightly golden. Let cool before serving.

Marshmallow Treats

Ingredients:

- **3 tablespoons** unsalted butter
- **1 package (10 oz)** mini marshmallows
- **6 cups** Rice Krispies cereal

Instructions:

1. In a large saucepan, melt the butter over low heat. Add the marshmallows and stir until completely melted.
2. Remove from heat and add the Rice Krispies, stirring until well coated.
3. Press the mixture into a greased 9x13-inch baking dish. Let cool before cutting into squares.

Chocolate Chip Banana Bread

Ingredients:

- **3 ripe bananas**, mashed
- **1/3 cup** melted butter
- **1/2 cup** granulated sugar
- **1 large** egg, beaten
- **1 teaspoon** vanilla extract
- **1 teaspoon** baking soda
- **1 pinch** salt
- **1 cup** all-purpose flour
- **1/2 cup** chocolate chips

Instructions:

1. Preheat the oven to 350°F (175°C). Grease a 4x8-inch loaf pan.
2. In a mixing bowl, mix the mashed bananas with melted butter. Stir in sugar, egg, and vanilla.
3. Mix in baking soda and salt, then add flour. Stir until just combined. Fold in chocolate chips.
4. Pour the batter into the prepared loaf pan and bake for 60-65 minutes, or until a toothpick comes out clean. Let cool before slicing.

Strawberry Shortcake

Ingredients:

- **1 pound** fresh strawberries, hulled and sliced
- **1/4 cup** granulated sugar
- **2 cups** all-purpose flour
- **1 tablespoon** baking powder
- **1/4 teaspoon** salt
- **1/4 cup** unsalted butter, softened
- **1 cup** heavy cream (plus more for serving)
- **1 teaspoon** vanilla extract

Instructions:

1. In a bowl, combine strawberries with sugar and set aside to macerate.
2. Preheat the oven to 425°F (220°C). In a mixing bowl, whisk together flour, baking powder, and salt. Cut in butter until crumbly.
3. Stir in heavy cream and vanilla until just combined. Turn dough onto a floured surface and knead gently. Roll out to about 1-inch thick and cut into rounds.
4. Place on a baking sheet and bake for 12-15 minutes until golden. Let cool.
5. To serve, split the shortcakes, layer with strawberries and whipped cream, and top with the other half.

Oatmeal Chocolate Chip Cookies

Ingredients:

- **1 cup** unsalted butter, softened
- **1 cup** brown sugar, packed
- **1/2 cup** granulated sugar
- **2 large** eggs
- **1 teaspoon** vanilla extract
- **1 1/2 cups** all-purpose flour
- **1 teaspoon** baking soda
- **1/2 teaspoon** salt
- **3 cups** rolled oats
- **1 cup** chocolate chips

Instructions:

1. Preheat the oven to 350°F (175°C). Line a baking sheet with parchment paper.
2. In a bowl, cream together the butter, brown sugar, and granulated sugar until light and fluffy. Beat in the eggs one at a time, then stir in the vanilla.
3. In another bowl, mix flour, baking soda, and salt. Gradually add to the creamed mixture. Stir in oats and chocolate chips.
4. Drop by tablespoonfuls onto the prepared baking sheet. Bake for 10-12 minutes until golden. Let cool before serving.